Music to My Ears

"Music to My Ears." By Marc Rivera. ISBN 978-1-947532-69-4 (softcover).

Published 2018 by Virtualbookworm.com Publishing Inc., P.O. Box 9949, College Station, TX , 77842, US.

Music to My Ears

by Marc Rivera
Illustrated by Debora Dyess

The world is a noisy place, but when you're a kid with autism like me, it's even NOISIER!

fireworkss

RINGGG!!

the
fire alarm
at school,

thunder-
storms

and
crowded
places

...make me cover my ears and cry.

Sometimes the loudness even makes me want to run away from all the sounds.

Oops!

Zooommm!

OMG!!

CRASH!!

RING!

RINGGG!!

Ding-Dong!

But there is one sound that does not bother me –

Monica, my music teacher, taught me about music.

She's the greatest!

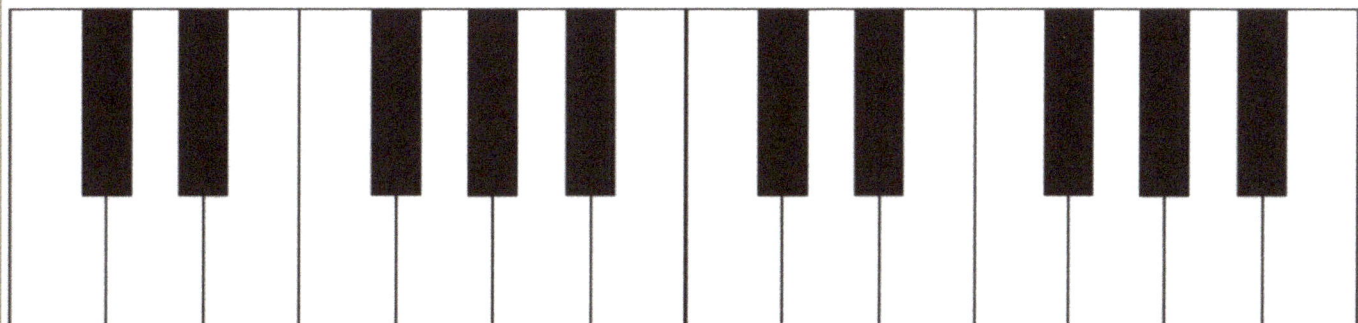

E G B D F

I learned to listen to slow music from many different musical instruments.

Monica also showed me videos of musicians playing slow music on their instruments, especially the piano.

The more I listened,

the more I became comfortable
with the beautiful sounds.

Now I can play piano for friends and family when they come to visit.

and even play at my birthday parties!

Playing music makes me happy.